12/07

ENERGY FOR THE FUTURE AND GLOBAL WARMING

FOSSIL FUELS

By Andrew Solway

Consultant: Suzy Gazlay, M.A.,
science curriculum resource teacher

Gareth Stevens
Publishing

Please visit our web site at: www.garethstevens.com
For a free color catalog describing Gareth Stevens Publishing's
list of high-quality books, call 1-800-542-2595 (USA) or
1-800-387-3178 (Canada).

Library of Congress Cataloging-in-Publication Data

Solway, Andrew.
    Fossil fuels / Andrew Solway.
       p. cm. — (Energy for the future and global warming)
    Includes index.
    ISBN: 978-0-8368-8399-2 (lib. bdg)
    ISBN: 978-0-8368-8408-1 (softcover)
    1. Fossil fuels—Juvenile literature. I. Title.
  TP318.S64   2008
  662'.62—dc22   2007008749

This edition first published in 2008 by
Gareth Stevens Publishing
A Weekly Reader® Company
1 Reader's Digest Road
Pleasantville, NY 10570-7000 USA

Copyright © 2008 by Gareth Stevens, Inc.

Editors: Geoff Barker and Sabrina Crewe
Designer: Keith Williams
Photo researchers: Sabrina Crewe and Rachel Tisdale
Illustrations: Stefan Chabluk and Keith Williams

Gareth Stevens editor: Carol Ryback
Gareth Stevens art direction and design: Tammy West
Gareth Stevens production: Jessica Yanke

Photo credits: SUNCOR Energy / Newscast: cover, title page, 13.
CORBIS: / James Marshall 6; / Roger Ressmeyer 28. BP p.l.c.: 9. NASA: 10.
Getty Images: / Robert Arnold 14. BLM Wyoming: 17. Library of Congress: 20.
istockphoto.com: 24. Exxon Valdez Oil Spill Trustee Council: 26.

Printed in the United States of America

1 2 3 4 5 6 7 8 9 11 10 09 08 07

CONTENTS

Cover photo: The Commerce City oil refinery, near Denver, Colorado, produces up to ninety thousand barrels of oil per day.

Words in **boldface** appear in the glossary or in the "Key Words" boxes within the chapters.

CHAPTER ONE

ENERGY AND GLOBAL WARMING

Do you hear your parents complain about the cost of electricity? Do they worry about the heating bill or the price of gas? When people talk about these things, they are talking about using energy.

What we do with energy

People use a lot of energy every day. We use energy to keep our homes warm or cool. We use energy every time we switch on a light or a computer. Growing food takes energy. It takes energy to get food to stores. You use energy when you cook food.

Factories that make things use energy. Everything from clothing to farm machinery takes energy to make.

We use a lot of energy for moving around, too. Cars, trucks, trains, and airplanes all need fuel to keep them going.

Where does our energy come from?

Today, most of our energy comes from petroleum, coal, and natural gas. Most people use the word "oil" when they talk about petroleum. When they are talking about natural gas, people often say just "gas." Oil, coal, and natural gas are known as **fossil fuels**.

Fossil fuels formed long ago from the remains of plants and animals. We use fossil fuels every day to make electricity. Fossil fuels also power our vehicles. Gasoline,

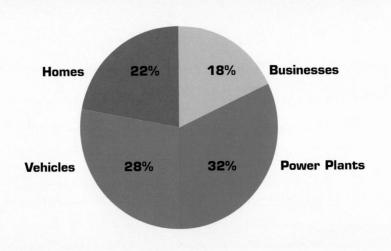

ENERGY USE IN THE UNITED STATES IN 2005

Homes **22%**   **18%** Businesses

Vehicles **28%**   **32%** Power Plants

This chart shows energy use in the United States. It shows how much was used by homes, businesses, **power plants**, and vehicles.

diesel, and other fuels are made from oil. Fossil fuels are used for heating and cooling homes, factories, and businesses.

The world's demand for energy

Every day, the world uses more energy. The global population is increasing. All these people are buying and using new machines that run on electricity.

North America and Europe already use lots of energy. Their energy needs are growing slowly.

Countries in Asia, Africa, and South America are beginning to need more fossil fuels. They are developing new industries. These industries need a lot of fuel.

The crowded Oshodi Market in Lagos, Nigeria. As the population grows, we need more and more energy.

Have we got enough?

The growing demand for energy uses up more fossil fuels. If we keep using more and more fossil fuels, they will run out. Fossil fuels are not **renewable**. We cannot renew — or easily replace — fossil fuels when they run out.

Running out

Experts argue about when fossil fuel supplies will be used up, but they agree that oil is likely to run out first.

Some experts think supplies of oil will start to decrease in just a few years. Others think it will be at least 2050 before oil begins to run out.

The natural gas supply will probably last longer than oil. Once we use up all the oil, we will start to use much more natural gas. The world's supply of natural gas may last for another 175 years.

Coal supplies will last longest of all. Most experts agree there is enough coal to last nearly three hundred years.

Where are the fossil fuels?

Some areas of the world have a lot of fossil fuels. Others have none. But all countries need fossil fuels. Without fossil fuels, daily life would change a lot. Power failures would happen frequently. There would be no fuel for vehicles, factories, heating, and cooking.

Today, the United States uses more oil than it produces. The U.S. must buy oil from other countries. Countries in the Middle East and South America produce more oil than they use. They sell their oil to other countries.

Wealthy nations, like the United States, can afford to

"Keeping America competitive requires affordable energy. And here we have a serious problem: America is addicted to oil, which is often imported from unstable parts of the world. The best way to break this addiction is through **technology**."

U.S. president George W. Bush, 2006

buy oil from other countries. The U.S. buys oil from around the world instead of reducing the amount used.

Pollution problems

When fossil fuels burn, they give off gases and smoke that cause **pollution**. In large towns and cities, the air is full of **emissions**. Emissions are waste products, such as

FOSSIL FUELS

GOOD THINGS	PROBLEMS
Cheapest and most reliable source of power available today	Major cause of pollution and global warming
Large supplies are still available	Not renewable once supplies are used up

gases and dust. The many vehicles in cities make emissions. In some places, these emissions cause smog. Smog is a thick, dirty fog that affects people's breathing. It can make them sick.

Burning fossil fuels also causes "acid rain." Sleet and snow can also be acidic. This moisture falls when fossil fuel gases mix with water vapor in clouds. Acid rain kills fish. It damages trees and other plants. In some areas, whole forests have been sickened by acid rain. It can also damage buildings and tombstones.

Greenhouse gases

The gases from fossil fuels are adding to another problem. The gases rise and form part of a blanket around Earth. The layer of gases traps heat in the atmosphere (air). We call these gases **greenhouse gases** because they trap heat the way a greenhouse does. The main greenhouse gas that comes from fossil fuels is carbon dioxide. Water vapor and **methane** are greenhouse gases, too.

The amounts of greenhouse gases in the air have increased in the last century. Scientists

The Texas City, Texas, refinery is the third largest oil refinery in the United States. Here, a worker performs a safety check.

GLOBAL WARMING

Global warming affects the entire Earth. Ice at the north and south poles is melting at a faster rate than ever before. The melting may cause a worldwide rise in sea levels. Higher sea levels will cause flooding in low areas along coasts.

As the world warms up, rainfall patterns change. Food crops may fail. Plants and animals that cannot adapt (adjust their lifestyles) to the changes may die out.

Arctic sea ice has melted a lot in recent years. Compare the amount of ice cover in 1979 (left) with the ice cover in 2005 (right). The area marked in red (right) shows where melting has occured.

believe this increase is causing Earth to get warmer. This changes the worldwide weather patterns, or climate. The climate change is called **global warming**.

Slowing global warming

If global warming continues at its current rate, it will change our world. To slow global warming, we need to burn less coal, oil, and

TWO TYPES OF ENERGY

Fossil fuels are primary (or first) sources of energy. Primary energy sources include fuels we burn to produce heat. Other primary sources of energy include moving water and the Sun. Flowing water creates energy when it pushes against objects. The Sun's energy warms us.

We use primary energy sources to make secondary sources of energy. They are called secondary sources of energy because they are made from something else. Electricity is a secondary source of energy. We can make it from fossil fuels, moving water, or solar (Sun) energy. Electricity is our main source of power. It powers many things.

natural gas. Using fewer fossil fuels will lower the amount of greenhouse gases (such as carbon dioxide) being pumped into the atmosphere. This will help reduce the greenhouse effect. But lowering the output of greenhouse gases will take a long time. It is important to start very soon.

KEY WORDS

fossil fuels: fuels formed over millions of years
global warming: the gradual warming of Earth's climate
greenhouse gases: substances in the air that trap heat energy
renewable: having a new or reusable supply of material constantly available for use

CHAPTER TWO

FUEL FROM THE ANCIENT PAST

Coal, oil, and natural gas were named fossil fuels for a reason. They formed from **fossils**. A fossil is the remains of an ancient (very old) plant or animal. Fossil fuels are the remains of animals or plants that lived millions of years ago. Like fossils, they are found in the ground. And like fossils, fossil fuels also take millions of years to form.

Long ago

Most of the world's coal formed 354 to 290 million years ago. This time period was before dinosaurs lived. At that time, all seven of Earth's continents were probably joined together in one giant continent, called "Pangea."

In some regions, large forests grew in **wetlands**.

Out of the wetlands

Coal slowly formed from the trees and other plants that lived in the wetlands. The process began about 300 million years ago. As plants died, they sank into the wetlands and began to rot. This rotting matter is the first stage of coal formation.

Dirt, water, and more plants piled up on top of the rotting trees. Time passed, and the bottom layers were buried even deeper. Heat from deep inside Earth warmed the bottom layers. More layers slowly built up on top. Their weight caused pressure on

OIL SANDS, TAR SANDS, SHALE

Some areas have huge **deposits** of oil close to the surface. The deposits are mixed in with sand and clay. They are known as **oil sands**, tar sands, or oil shale. Oil in these deposits does not look like oil from deep underground. Oil in oil sands is thick and heavy. Most oil sands are in Canada and Venezuela. The U.S. has the largest deposits of oil shale in the world. It is very expensive to **extract** (remove) oil from oil sands. Enormous machinery is required.

Canada's Athabasca oil sands in Alberta contain the biggest oil sand deposits in the world. Gigantic diggers are used.

the lower layers. Deep below, the heat and pressure kept building up.

After millions of years, these layers became hard. Some of these layers formed the coal we dig out of the ground today.

Under the ocean

Seventy percent of Earth is covered by ocean. Unlike coal, oil and most natural gas formed under the oceans

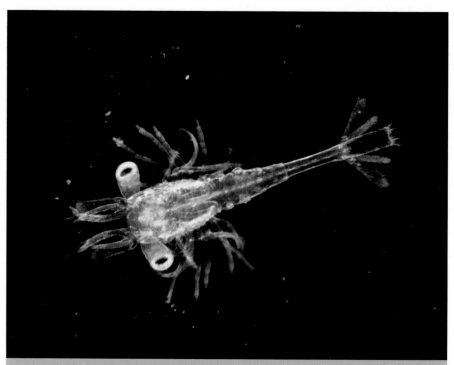

The oceans contain plankton (tiny ocean plants and animals). Plankton that live today are very similar to plankton that formed oil and gas deposits.

instead of on land. Natural gas also formed near coal.

Oil and natural gas formed from tiny, floating ocean plants and animals called plankton. As the plankton died, they sank to the ocean floor. There, they mixed with sand and mud. The plankton were buried, squashed, and heated. Other layers of sand, mud, and plankton formed above. The weight of these layers caused pressure. Heat from inside Earth warmed the buried layers. Heat and pressure turned the plankton into oil or natural gas.

This process took millions of years. Oil and natural gas formed in the deep rock

TYPES OF COAL

Not all coal is the same. Some types of coal are harder than others. Some burn hotter than others. The softest and "youngest" coal — lignite — formed closest to the surface. It is not as hard as the coals found deeper down. Sub-bituminous coal is harder and burns hotter than lignite. The United States has a lot of sub-bituminous coal. But it has even more bituminous coal, which is older and buried a little deeper. Bituminous coal also burns hotter than the "younger" coals. The coal that formed first and deepest is called anthracite. It is the oldest type of coal and burns hottest of all. It is rare in the United States.

layers. Sometimes, oil and natural gas bubbles up through the rock layers. But most oil and natural gas stays trapped underground.

Some oil and natural gas deposits lie deep below the ocean floors. Other deposits — or pockets — of oil and natural gas are beneath dry ground that was once under water many centuries ago.

KEY WORDS

deposit: a natural pocket of fossil fuel or other valuable minerals
fossil: the remains of an ancient plant or animal preserved in rock
oil sands: deposits of oil mixed with sand and clay
wetlands: areas that are covered in shallow water

CHAPTER THREE

OUT OF THE GROUND

Coal was the first important fossil fuel. People began to use a lot of coal in the 1700s.

Mining coal

Coal is **mined** (removed) from the ground. Layers of rock that hold coal are called seams. Some coal seams are close to the surface. Miners can dig a large pit at the surface to remove coal from these seams.

Most coal is found deep underground. Miners use machines to dig a shaft — a tunnel that goes down to the coal seam. They use other equipment to extract the coal from the seam.

Coal is crushed into small lumps when it is mined.

Small pieces of coal are easier to transport and use. Railroad trains transport coal across the United States. Coal can also be moved through a pipeline. To move through a pipeline, the coal is first crushed into small pieces and mixed with oil or water. This thick, black mixture is pumped through a pipeline.

Oil and natural gas

Oil and natural gas deposits are usually found deep underground. Workers reach the deposits by drilling **wells** — holes — down to the fuel. The oil or gas is not in a big puddle or bubble. Tiny holes, called pores, within the rock hold the oil or natural gas. The fuel is usually under

At this open-pit mine in Wyoming, coal is dug from the surface. Most coal is mined deep underground.

pressure because it is trapped so deep between the rock layers. A well that reaches a deposit releases that pressure. Fuel rushes to the surface, where it is collected. As oil or gas is removed from a well, the pressure down below slowly falls. After a while, no more fuel rushes to the surface.

Oil industry **engineers** use several methods to remove the most oil and natural gas from deposits. One process pumps carbon dioxide into the well through a second well drilled nearby. The carbon dioxide spreads through the rocks. It pushes oil up and out through the first well.

KEY WORDS

engineer: someone who uses math and science knowledge to design and operate machines
mine: to remove natural products from the ground; also, an area that holds those natural products
well: a hole dug into the ground to reach a natural deposit, such as water, oil, or natural gas

17

CHAPTER FOUR

POWERING THE WORLD

Until 1901, only small pockets of oil had been discovered in the United States. That year, a huge oil deposit was found in Texas. Within a few years, oil had become an important fuel. People began using vehicles that ran on oil. Power plants began using oil to produce electricity. Oil production became big business.

Producing oil

Crude oil (oil straight from the ground) is not pure. It is a thick, lumpy, smelly fluid. "Heavy" crude contains a lot of sulfur and asphalt. It is thick, dark, and sticky. "Light" crude is pale brown and flows easily. Most crude oil is a mixture of the two.

Crude oil must be refined (made pure). It needs to be split into usable substances. Crude oil is refined and separated in a large plant called an oil refinery.

The separated parts of refined crude oil become different products. The main products are gasoline, diesel, and heating oil.

Natural gas

Until the mid-1900s, natural gas was not as important a fuel as coal and oil. Gas was too hard to transport. Since then, however, the demand for natural gas has grown. Companies have found ways to move natural gas around the world. They use special ships and pipelines.

Most crude oil is used to make fuels for vehicles. The rest is used to produce many other products. Asphalt is used to make surfaces for roads, parking lots, and playgrounds. Lighter oils and greases help all kinds of engines run smoothly. Oil is also used in polishing waxes and waterproof coatings. Chemicals from oil are used in plastics and clothing. Ink, deodorant, crayons, and bubble gum all contain oil. Your soft drink bottle is also a petroleum product.

Products made from oil

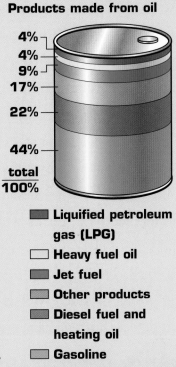

4%
4%
9%
17%
22%
44%
total
100%

■ **Liquified petroleum gas (LPG)**
□ **Heavy fuel oil**
■ **Jet fuel**
□ **Other products**
■ **Diesel fuel and heating oil**
□ **Gasoline**

It is not always possible to transport gas in pipelines. A lot of natural gas is transported in tankers (ships with tanks). First, the natural gas is purified (made pure). Then, it is cooled until it becomes a liquid. It is called liquified natural gas (LNG).

Oil is measured in 42-gallon (159-liter) barrels. The barrel chart shows the amount (percentage) of crude oil used to produce various products.

The LNG can be moved from place to place in tankers.

Today, the United States uses natural gas for about one-quarter of its energy needs. More than half the homes in the United States use natural gas for heating. Overall, however, industries in the United States use about 32 percent of the natural gas produced.

Natural gas is mostly methane. It is separated into different gases at processing plants. Methane burns well and with a clean flame. It has no smell. The familiar "rotten egg" smell is added so that we can detect (find) gas leaks. In cities, methane is piped into homes. It is used as a fuel for heating and cooking.

Other gases found in natural gas are propane and butane. People use propane for their barbecue grills. Butane is often added to propane and to gasoline.

Using coal

Coal can be used without much processing. It can be used in large or small lumps or as a fine powder.

THE FIRST POWER PLANT

In 1882, inventor Thomas Edison built the first U.S. power plant in New York City. The Pearl Street Central Power Station supplied electricity to homes that had electric lights.

Thomas Edison at Edison Machine Works, West Orange, New Jersey, in 1906.

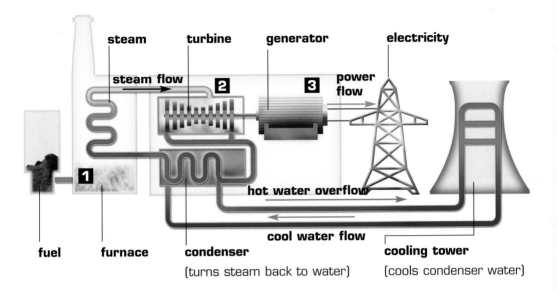

steam   turbine   generator   electricity

steam flow   **2**   **3**   power flow

1

hot water overflow

cool water flow

fuel   furnace   condenser   cooling tower
(turns steam back to water)   (cools condenser water)

What happens in a power plant?
A furnace burns fuel (1). The heat changes water into steam. The steam feeds into a turbine (2) — a series of many-bladed fans. Steam makes the turbine spin. The spinning turbine spins the generator (3). The generator can be either a spinning coil of wire surrounded by a large magnet or a large magnet that spins around a wire coil. This action produces electricity.

For many years, people burned coal on fires to heat their homes. Coal was also important as a fuel for locomotives in the days before people had cars. In some parts of the world, people still use coal fires and coal stoves.

Most U.S. power plants burn coal to make steam. The steam turns large machines called **turbines**. The turbines power generators that make electricity. Coal produces more than half of the electricity Americans use.

Around the world

Every year, the world uses huge amounts of fossil fuels.

In 2005, the world used almost 11 billion tons (10 billion tonnes) of oil, natural gas, and coal. The two biggest users are the United States and China. The United States uses almost one-quarter of all fossil fuels. China uses less oil and natural gas than the United States, but it uses more than one-third of all of the world's coal.

Canada uses more energy for every person than the United States, China, or Mexico. How can this be?

Canada has a cold climate. Its people are spread out over a large area. They often travel far every day. But Canada has a lot of fossil fuels. Energy is cheap there. Canadians use a lot of energy in their homes and industries.

2005 energy use per person in kilowatt-hours/megajoules (kWh/mJ)

Canada 122,504 kWh/441,013 mJ

U.S. 100,523 kWh/361,884 mJ

Mexico 18,463kWh/66,468 mJ

China 12,093 kWh/43,533 mJ

KEY WORDS

power plant: a factory that produces electricity

refine: to make pure by removing or separating unwanted substances

turbine: an engine powered by a flowing fluid, such as moving air. Turbines have large, spinning blades. Turbines power generators that produce electricity.

kilowatt-hours (kWh): a unit of energy output equal to 3.6 million joules. 1 joule is a unit of force needed to move 3.6 ounces (102 grams) about 3.3 feet (1 meter).

CHAPTER FIVE

THE FUTURE FOR FOSSIL FUELS

Sooner or later, fossil fuel supplies will start running out. People all over the world are thinking about different ways to save energy and new ways to make it.

New forms of energy

We need to use more types of renewable energy. These energy sources will never run out. Wind power and solar power (energy from the Sun) are freely available. Biofuels, fuels made from plant or animal waste, are renewable. We must find easy ways to use all these forms of energy.

Efficient energy

For now, however, we still need to use fossil fuels. Other

FUEL SOURCES USED WORLDWIDE IN 2003

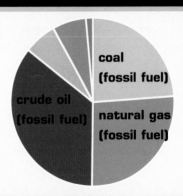

- Coal — 23.9%
- Natural gas — 26.3%
- Crude oil — 35.4%
- Nuclear power — 6.4%
- Hydroelectric power — 6.6%
- Geothermal and other — 1.4%

coal (fossil fuel)

crude oil (fossil fuel)

natural gas (fossil fuel)

This chart shows the different fuels used to generate the world's electricity in 2003. As you can see, fossil fuels were used most often.

ENERGY PHANTOMS

Any device with a remote control uses energy twenty-four hours a day, seven days a week. Televisions, CD and DVD players, and other devices with "instant-on" controls are always "on" — even when they are "off." Coffeemakers with timers stay on throughout the night before they make coffee. Most answering machines and computers never really shut down. Such energy use is called "phantom load." Fossil fuels usually produce phantom load electricity.

Experts say 6 percent of the energy Americans use in their homes is phantom-load energy. That's a lot of energy. How much fossil fuel would it take to produce that amount of energy? Believe it or not, that same amount of fossil fuel could supply electricity to Greece, Peru, and Vietnam all at once!

Shutting off a computer's power strip every night is one way to save a lot of fossil fuel energy — and money! Most people do not do that, however.

sources of energy do not yet give us the fuel we need. But we must reduce pollution and slow global warming. We can do this by making better use of fossil fuels.

We can find new ways to save fossil fuels. We also need to use that energy in better ways. Using energy well is **efficient**. It also saves fuel and money. Efficient use of fuel reduces pollution and global warming. We have already found some ways to use fossil fuels efficiently.

Clean and not so clean

Some fossil fuels are cleaner than others. Natural gas burns very cleanly. It produces much less **carbon dioxide** than other fossil fuels. Only about 5 percent of **emissions** from a natural gas power plant are made of carbon dioxide.

Oil produces more pollution than natural gas. The worst polluter of all is coal. Emissions from a coal power plant are between 10 and 15 percent carbon dioxide. Coal also produces wastes that include sulfur, nitrogen, and mercury. These chemicals pollute the air, land, and water.

Scrubbing them clean

Industries have done a lot to reduce the pollution from coal. New power plants "scrub" the gases given off by coal. Scrubbing cleans the gases before they go into the air. Filters and chemical traps on smokestacks remove most of the **pollutants** from smoke.

Fossil fuels are burned in **furnaces** (fuel burners). Good furnace design can help reduce pollution. Fossil fuels burned in efficient furnaces produce less pollution.

Capturing carbon dioxide

We can scrub pollutants from fossil fuels. Can we scrub carbon dioxide from

OIL EATERS

In 1989, the *Exxon Valdez* oil tanker ran aground on the southern coast of Alaska. The ship spilled nearly 11 million gallons (42 million liters) of crude oil. The oil polluted nearly 2,000 miles (3,200 kilometers) of the coast. It killed thousands of seabirds and other animals.

Some of the cleanup crews used bacteria (tiny life forms with only one cell) to rid the shoreline of oil. These bacteria already lived along the Alaskan coast. Scientists found ways to make the bacteria grow faster than usual. The bacteria that were spread on the beaches fed on the spilled oil. They removed some of the pollution naturally.

Crews work to clean up oil from the *Exxon Valdez* accident. Oil still pollutes some Alaskan beaches today — nearly twenty years after the spill.

FUEL EFFICIENT FAMILY

What would happen if every family in the United States left their car at home for one trip a week? It would save about 27.5 million tons (25 million tonnes) of carbon dioxide emissions each year!

fuels, too? The answer is yes. Capturing carbon dioxide stops it from going into the air. Scientists and engineers are working on ways to capture carbon dioxide. They use chemicals that join with the carbon dioxide to extract (remove) it. Other materials absorb (soak up) the gas.

Capturing carbon dioxide is just half the problem. It also needs to be stored somewhere safe. There are several places that may be used in the future. Carbon dioxide can be pumped into coal seams that are too deep to mine. The gas can also be pumped into an aquifer. An aquifer is an underground area that holds water. Some acquifers could store carbon dioxide gas.

Better power plants

The fossil fuels we have left will last longer if we use less energy. One way to use less energy is to be more efficient. In most power plants, only about one-third of the energy from fuel becomes electricity. The rest of the energy is lost as heat. Today, new kinds of power plants are being built. They are designed to lose less heat.

This coal gasification plant in Plaquemine, Louisiana, is one of the new kinds of power plants. It produces "clean" energy.

More energy, less waste

One new type of power plant is very efficient. It combines two ways of using the heat from fuel to make energy. A combined-cycle plant uses natural gas in its turbine to make electricity. The waste gas from the gas turbine is very hot. It heats water to make steam. The steam powers a steam turbine. Then, another turbine makes electricity from the same natural gas!

Another new type of power plant uses coal to produce the gas for the combined-cycle method. It is called a **coal gasification plant.** Gasification is the process of making gas. First, the plant breaks coal down into gas. That gas is burned to make electricity. The coal gasification process is much cleaner and more efficient than simply burning coal. Much less fossil fuel energy gets wasted.

Fossil fuels' future

In the near future, we should start using more renewable energy sources. Some new cars will be designed to run on renewable fuels. New energy sources may provide power for many homes, too.

Fossil fuels will probably be burned in power plants for a long time, however. Large industries, such as steel making, will also continue to use fossil fuels. But future power plants and factories that burn fuels efficiently will be built. They will use less fuel and make less pollution. Power plants and factories may capture and store carbon dioxide underground.

Fossil fuels will be used for years into the future. We must learn to use them more wisely, however. They fulfill and important energy need.

KEY WORDS

carbon dioxide: a gas released by a decaying plant or a burning fuel. Too much carbon dioxide in the air helps increase the rate of global warming. Plants use carbon dioxide to grow and produce food.

efficient: working well and without much waste

emission: a waste, such as carbon dioxide given off by fossil fuel burning, that usually adds to pollution

pollutant: something that pollutes (makes dirty) air, water, or land

GLOSSARY

coal gasification plant: a power plant that breaks down coal into gases to use for making electricity

crude oil: petroleum oil before it is refined

deposit: a natural store of a fossil fuel or other mineral

efficient: working well and without much waste

emission: a waste product, such as carbon dioxide, that usually adds to air, land, or water pollution

extract: to remove from another substance

fossil fuels: fuels formed in the ground over millions of years, including coal, oil, and natural gas deposits

furnace: a device that burns fuel

global warming: the gradual warming of Earth's climate

greenhouse gases: substances in the atmosphere that trap heat energy

methane: an important fuel and a greenhouse gas. Natural gas is mostly methane.

pollution: making land, air, or water dirty

power plant: a factory that produces electricity

refine: to make pure by removing or separating unwanted substances

renewable: having a new or reusable supply of material constantly available

technology: the use of science, knowledge, and tools to improve methods or devices

TOP EIGHT ENERGY SOURCES

The following list highlights the major fuel sources of the twenty-first century. It also lists some advantages and disadvantages of each:

	Advantages	Disadvantages
Biofuels	renewable energy source; widely available from a number of sources, including farms, restaurants, and everday garbage	fossil fuels often used to grow farm crops; requires special processing facilities that run on fossil fuels in order to produce usable biofuel
Fossil fuels: coal, oil, petroleum	used by functioning power plants worldwide; supports economies	limited supplies; emit greenhouse gases; produce toxic wastes; must often be transported long distances
Geothermal energy	nonpolluting; renewable; free source	only available in localized areas; would require redesign of heating systems
Hydrogen (fuel cells)	most abundant element in the universe; nonpolluting	production uses up fossil fuels; storage presents safety issues
Nuclear energy	produces no greenhouse gases; produces a lot of energy from small amounts of fuel	solid wastes remain dangerous for centuries; limited life span of power plants
Solar power	renewable; produces no pollutants; free source	weather and climate dependent; solar cells expensive to manufacture
Water power	renewable resource; generally requires no additional fuel	requires flowing water, waves, or tides; can interfere with view; dams may destroy large natural areas and disrupt human settlements
Wind power	renewable; nonpolluting; free source	depends on weather patterns; depends on location; endangers bird populations

RESOURCES

Books

Graham, Ian.
Fossil Fuels: A Resource Our World Depends On.
Managing Our Resources (series).
Heinemann Infosearch (2004)

Saunders, Nigel
and Steven Chapman.
Fossil Fuel. Energy Essentials/
Freestyle Express (series).
Raintree (2005)

Web Sites

www.eia.doe.gov/kids/
Follow the related links for
a wealth of energy information.

*www.energyquest.ca.gov/saving_
energy/index.html*
Read Professor Questor's energy-
saving tips.

Publisher's note to educators and parents: Our editors have carefully reviewed these Web sites to ensure that they are suitable for children. Many Web sites change frequently, however, and we cannot guarantee that a site's future contents will continue to meet our high standards of quality and educational value. Be advised that children should be closely supervised whenever they access the Internet.

INDEX